Colin McNaughton's
ABC
and
THINGS
D1737399

A

is for All at sea

DOUBLEDAY & COMPANY INC.,
·GARDEN CITY·NEW YORK·

The Benn Book Collection
Published by Doubleday & Company Inc.,
Garden City, New York

First edition in the United States
of America
Printed in England

Library of Congress
Catalog Card Number 77-71993

Library of Congress Cataloging
in Publication Data
McNaughton, Colin
Colin McNaughton's ABC and 1 2 3

The 2 works were first published
separately under titles:
ABC and things and 1 2 3 and things.
"The Benn Book Collection"
Summary: Illustrations of ridiculous
situations introduce the letters of the
alphabet and numbers from one to twenty.
[1. Alphabet books. 2. Counting books]
I. McNaughton, Colin. 1 2 3 and things. 1977.
II. Title. III. Title; ABC and 1 2 3.
PZ7.M23256Co3[E] 77-71993

ISBN 0-385-13273-5 Trade
0-385-13614-5 Prebound

B

is for Bending the rules

C
is for Crime wave

D

is for Dead end

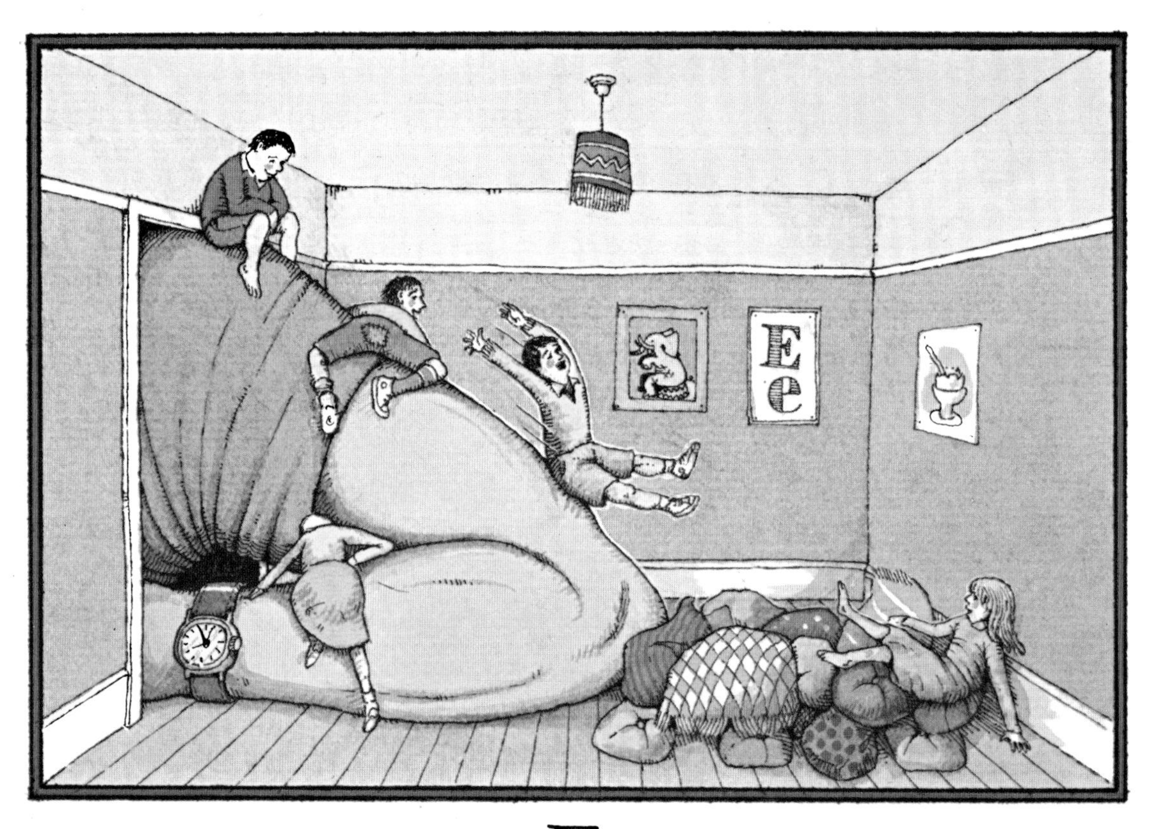

E

is for Elbow room

F

is for Flying off the handle

G
is for Gate-crashing

H

is for Hay fever

I

is for In the soup

J

is for Jumping the line

K
is for Keeping mum

L

is for Letting off steam

M

is for Moving house

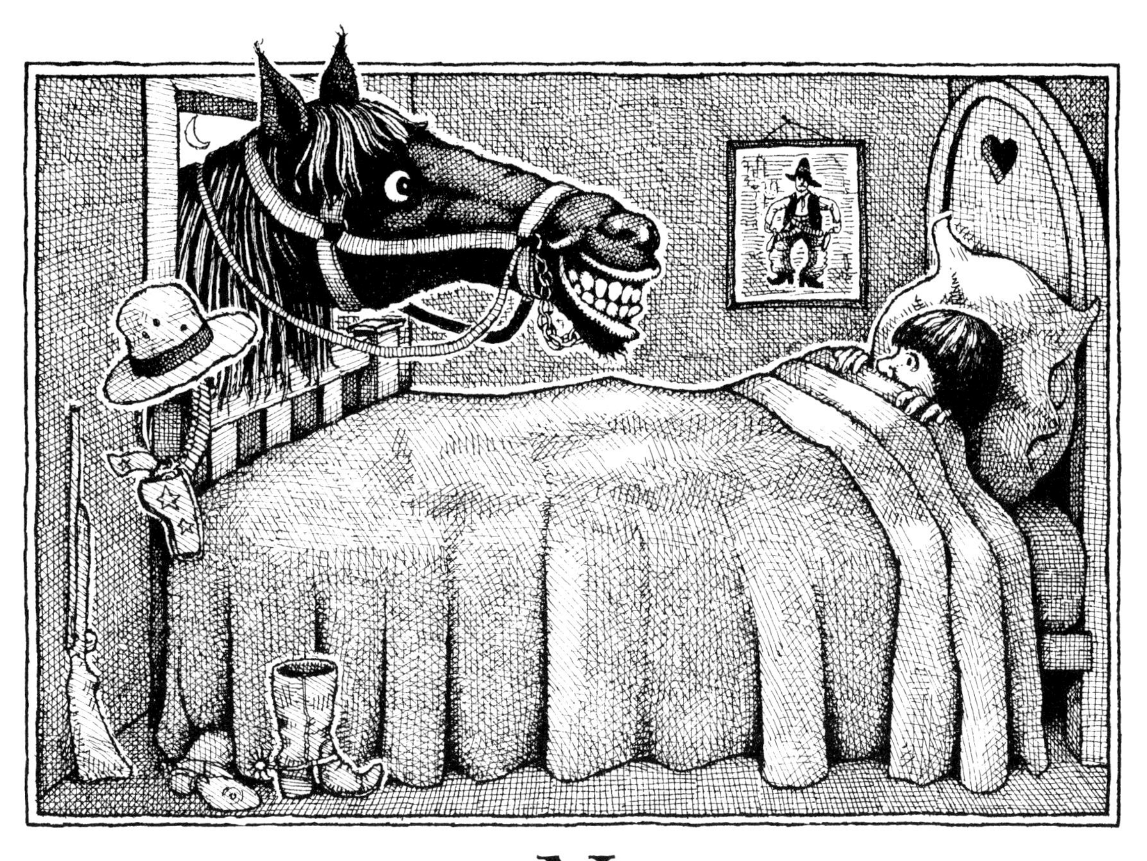

N
is for Nightmare

O
is for Over the moon

P

is for Potatoes in their jackets

Q

is for Quiet as a mouse

R

is for Running a temperature

S
is for Storm in a teacup

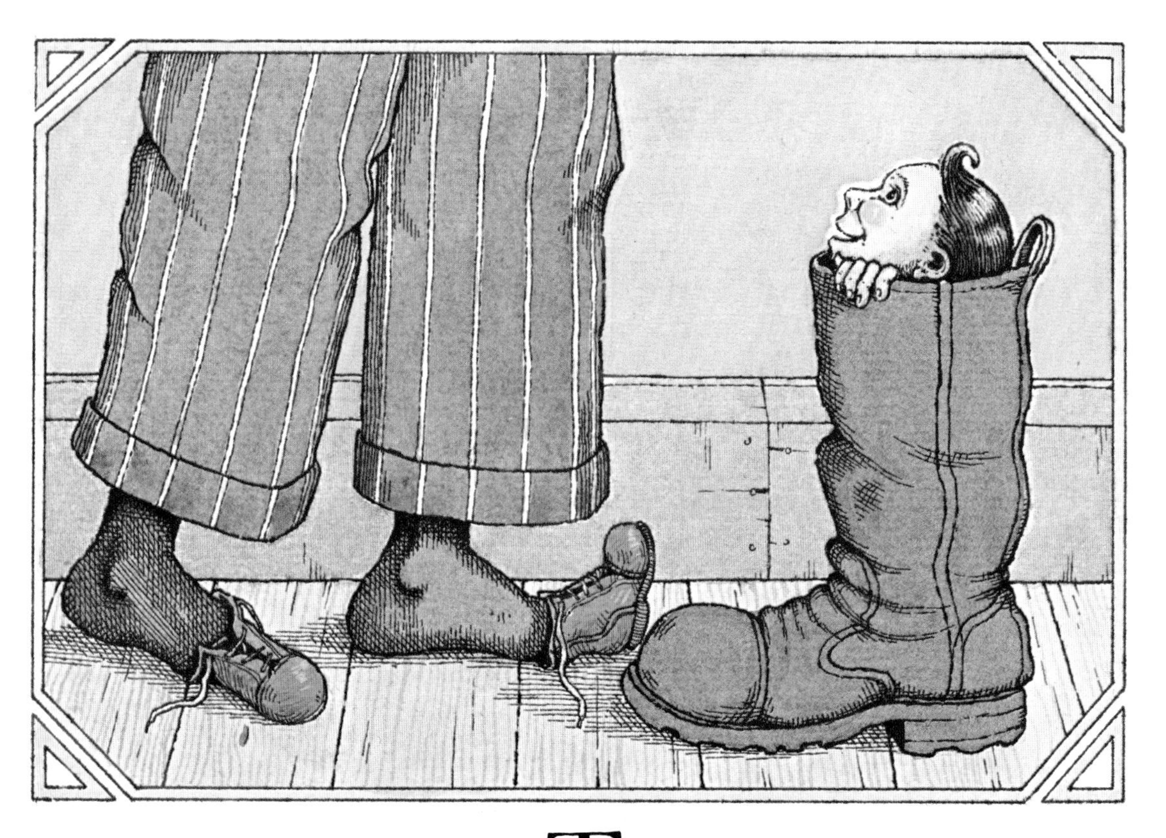

T

is for Too big for his boots

U

is for Under the weather

V

is for Visiting card

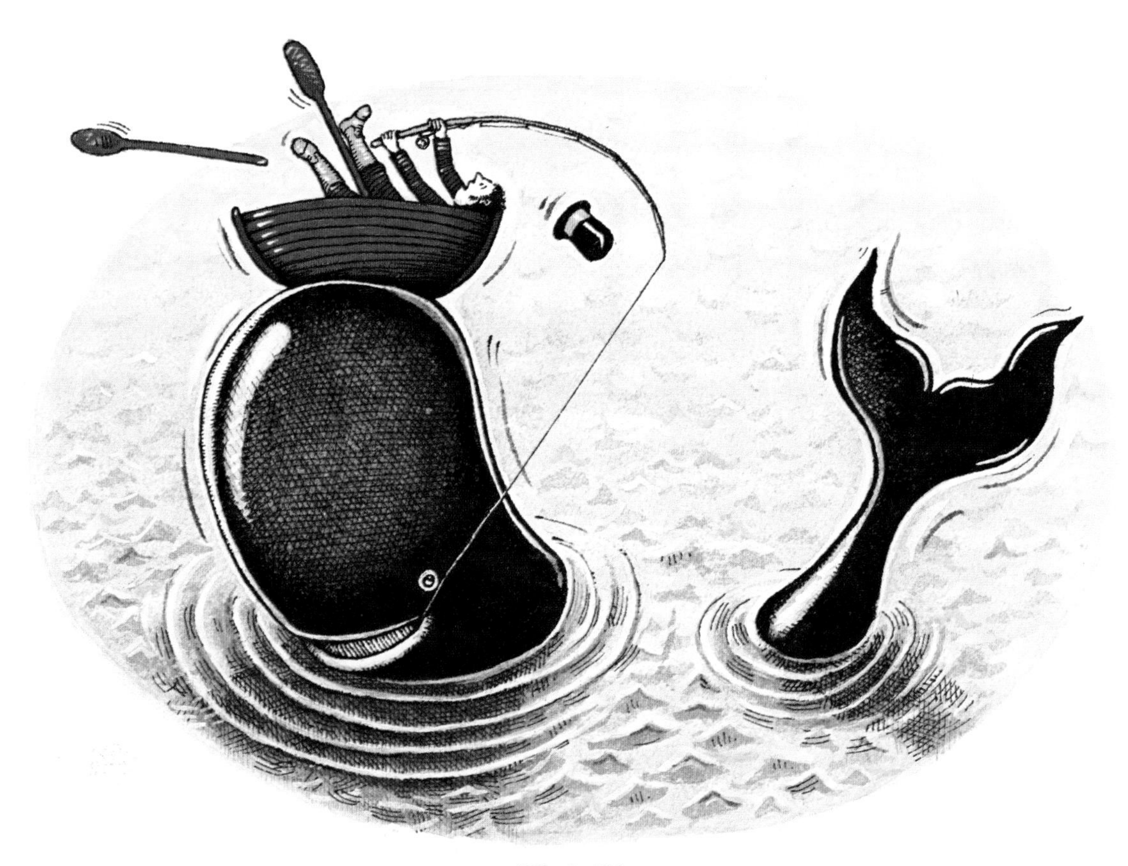

W
is for a Whale of a time

X

is for X marks the spot

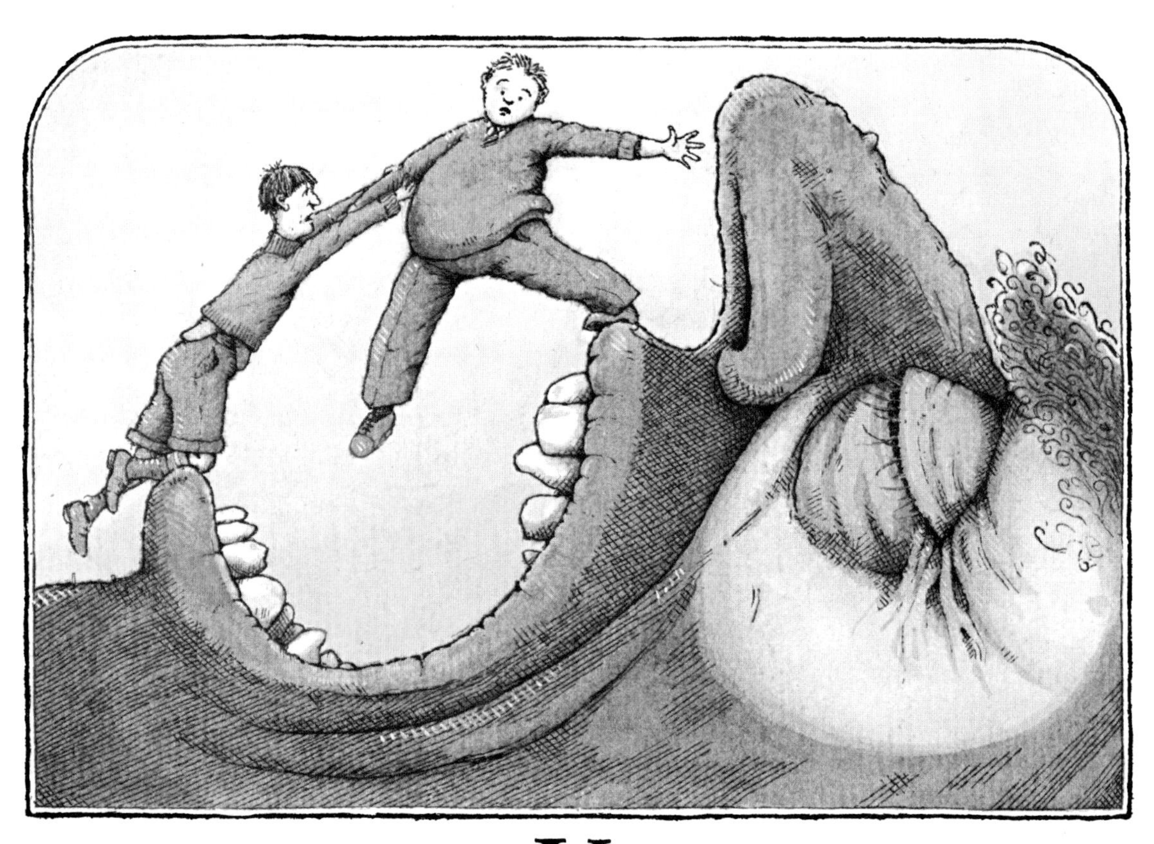

Y

is for Yawning gap

Z
is for Zipping along

A B C D E F G H I J K L M N
a b c d e f g h i j k l m n

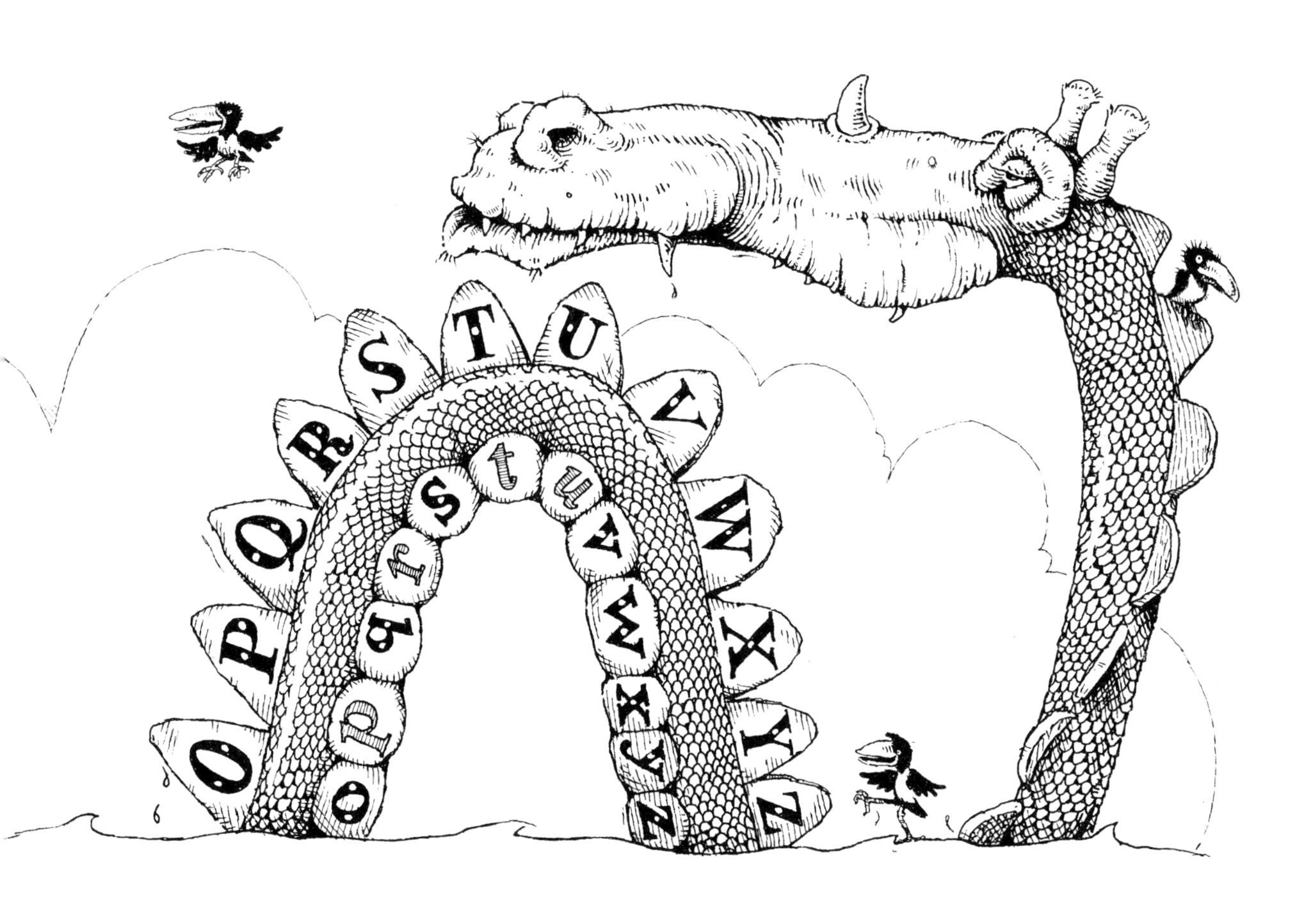
O P Q R S T U V W X Y Z
o p q r s t u v w x y z

Colin McNaughton's
123
AND
THINGS
Ernest Benn

1 One on the run from a vast cream bun

2 Two marabou say how do you do

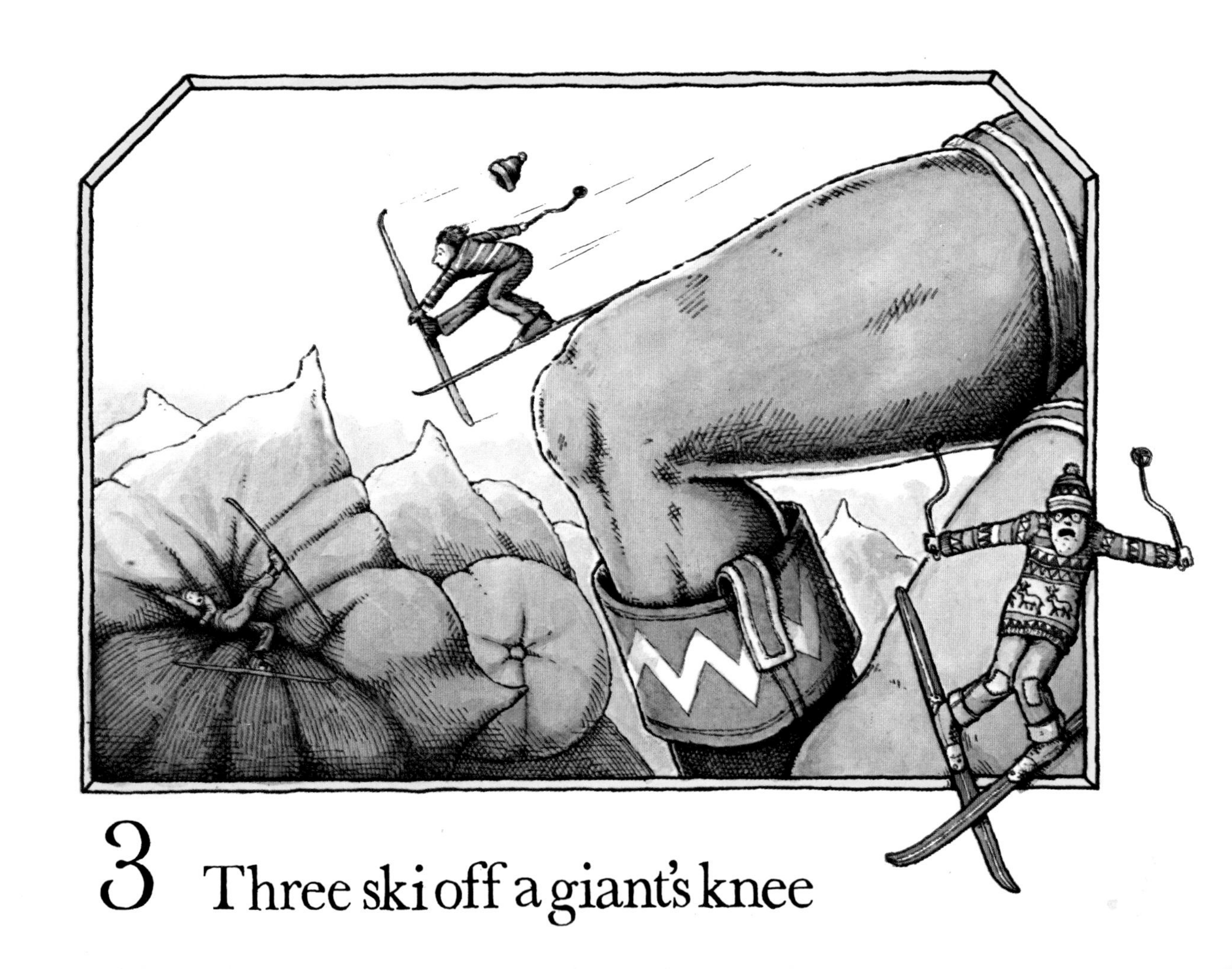

3 Three ski off a giant's knee

4 Four in awe of a dinosaur

5 Five on a drive - will they survive?

6 Six do tricks on candlesticks

7 Seven in heaven in deepest Devon

8 Eight, late, await their fate

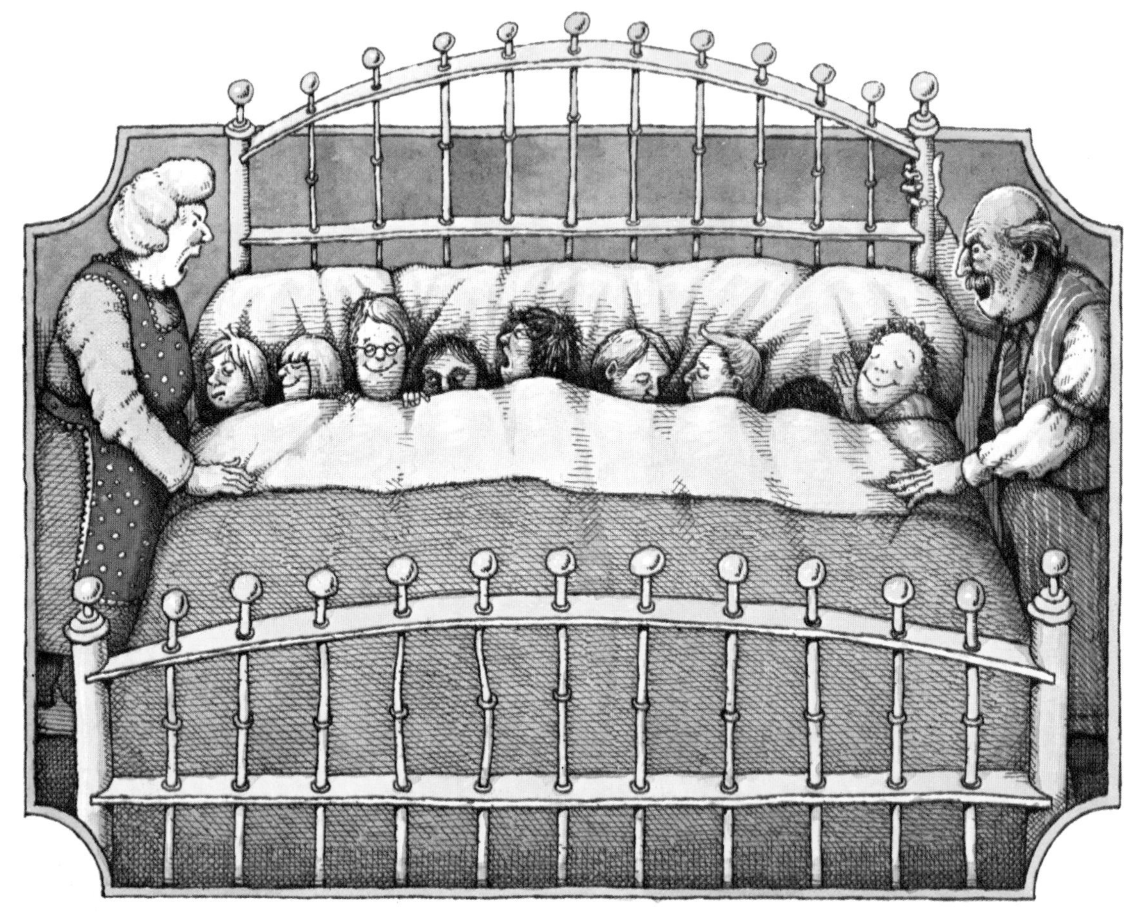

9 Nine decline to rise and shine

10 Ten young men in a lion's den

11 Eleven bears without any cares

12 Twelve baboons in blue balloons

13 Thirteen rats in old men's hats

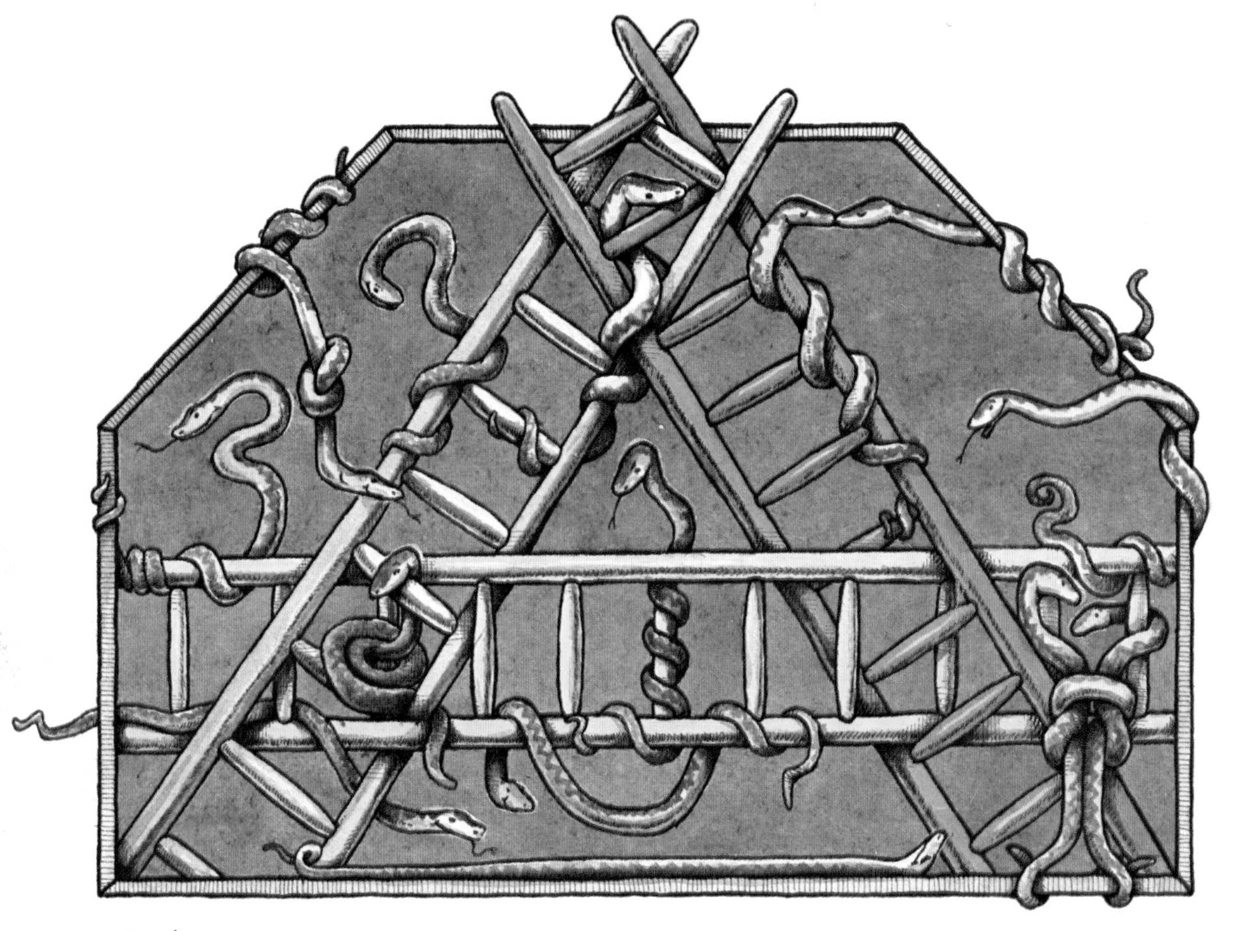

14 Fourteen adders play snakes and ladders

15 Fifteen boys make a monstrous noise

16 Sixteen birds say absurd words

halloo
NEEZ
nurge
SPLONG
wump
Sprott
fudge
PLINGE
PARP

17 Seventeen pigs in various wigs

18 Eighteen fly from a hot mince pie

19 Nineteen girls all diving for pearls

20 Twenty climb for the very first time

50,084 Fifty thousand and eighty four

could not believe just what they saw